MAKE YOUR HOUSE A HOME PLACE

HOW TO ENJOY YOUR LIFE FOR MORE FUN, ADVENTURE AND SUCCESS

JOHN RIGGLE

Year of the Book

135 Glen Avenue

Glen Rock, Pennsylvania 17327

ISBN 13: 978-1-942430-28-5

ISBN 10: 1-942430-28-0

Library of Congress Control Number: 2015949146

Contents

Preface

While living in Richmond, Virginia I developed a good relationship with a friend who became an advisor and mentor.

In one of our learning moments he pulled me aside and said "Riggle, do you know where you are going?"

"Yes sir, I think I do," I replied.

"Well, then are you enjoying the journey?"

So it is with life. Learning to enjoy the journey can be the most important thing you ever accomplish no matter how hard it may seem or how difficult the path.

This book is designed to help you develop *joy* in the path you take.

It all begins with your right to choose.

Chapter 1
The Power of Choice

There are few things we don't get to choose: our heritage, our birthplace, the color of our eyes, the body we were born into.

That said, the right to choose—to improve or not to improve—is a divine right! What we do with what we have been given determines how happy and fulfilled we can be.

I liken this right to a funnel. Let's call it the *Choose the Right* (CTR) funnel.

When you were first born you had few choices. You could cry or poop your diaper. You couldn't even roll over in bed. Then you began to grow. First you could roll over, then scoot on your belly, then crawl and eventually walk.

You learned to make choices and sometimes mistakes. You began to learn that good choices yield rewards and bad ones hurt. You learned not to fall from high places or put your hand on a hot stove.

The more good choices you made, the more opportunities were presented to you to make newer and better choices.

Just like entering a funnel, the small end was restrictive. But by going the *right* direction… things began to open up!

Soon you were 16 and driving a car. Your world began to expand just like the mouth of the funnel. You could go new places, see new things. As long as you made the right choices more opportunities to make new and better choices occurred.

For some, the decision is to *Choose the Wrong* (CTW) funnel. When we make the wrong choices the funnel begins to head back to the small end.

For example, you might decide to drink and drive. If you're lucky you only get caught by the police, and decide to switch back to the CTR funnel. But if you choose the CTW funnel things begin to close in on you... a second violation loses your ability to travel as easily, and a third takes you to the small end of the funnel where your only choice might be... "Do I sit on the stainless steel toilet or the bunk bed in my small room with bars and a roommate not of my choosing?" Bad choices lead to fewer choices, and just like the small end of the funnel you can end up restricted to almost no choice.

These choices guide your life and its outcome. While your opportunity may vary based on your circumstance you always have a *right* to choose the right way—even if it seems as though that way is more difficult.

If you accept this right of choice, you will come to understand that in almost every case your choices will yield consequence of some sort. While you may be free to make a choice, you are not free to choose its consequence.

In almost every case when this freedom of choice is restricted it leads to conflict and sometimes war. Think about it. The American Revolution, the French revolution, World War I and World War II were all a result of fighting over the right to choose. Almost every war ever fought was due to a question of choice! Even the war in heaven where Satan wanted to restrict choice turned into a battle over this divine right.

While it seems like some people get away with restricting choice eventually it catches them. It just takes time and the consequence may not be fully visible.

What about those who remain trapped in this battle of choice?

Are they really trapped?

Even those caught with limited choice almost always have a choice. True, they may not like the consequence of their choice but they can choose to take the highest road possible.

What about those born to unfortunate circumstance?

It is interesting that many children in difficult and minimal existence can be so happy despite their environment.

In many cases, *they don't know what they don't know.*

They make the most of their environment and learn to play and create.

They may create a soccer ball from plastic bottles or play ball with a stick.

Even "kick the can" can be fun!

How did the early American pioneers ever survive with no television or video gaming? They were unaware of these potential entertainments so they toiled, sang and danced. Others who are blessed with almost everything are often upset because they want more and they may have a false sense of entitlement.

Abraham Lincoln once said, "Most folks are as happy as they make up their minds to be."

The real question is:
"What do we do with what we are given?"
How do we build a pattern of *Choose the Right?*

There was a man in the 1800s named Parley who, while proselytizing, was unjustly forced to spend the night in jail. He was scheduled to be transferred to another jail the next morning. The magistrate warned him not to try to escape during the process because the sheriff had a bull dog named Stu that could take any man down.

That next morning during the transfer Parley thanked the sheriff for the good meal and a warm night's stay and said, "I must be on my way." He then proceeded to swiftly run away.

The sheriff was shocked at his action and finally recovered by yelling, "Go get him, Stu. Go get him!" The dog ran after the fleeing Parley, growling and barking loudly.

Just as Stu was about to overtake him, Parley stopped in his tracks and pointed to the woods ahead. "Go get him, Stu. Go get him!"

The bulldog ran straight ahead into the woods and Parley ran away safe and sound!

The lesson in this true story is simply that even though the dog had a great sense of direction he had no real goal.

In our lives we set so-called goals such as: "I will do better" or "I will be smarter" about something. These efforts give us better direction but lack the qualities of a real set of goals.

Just like the dog… we may be going in the right direction, but we need to know what we're aiming for (like the seat of Parley's pants).

So what must we do to set goals?

A commonly used acronym holds the answer… **S.M.A.R.T.**

S means specific.

M means measurable.

A means achievable.

R means a reach.

T means time-bound.

For a goal to be meaningful it needs each of these elements.

Specific refers to a defined outcome. For the sake of example let's use a 15% increase over last year's income.

That kind of outcome is measurable.

If 15% is an achievable number you will try to reach it.

If it is too small, you ignore it.

Too large, you won't even try.

If it makes you reach you will develop strategies to get there. If it is time-bound you will begin to target your behavior with benchmarks.

Hence a goal of a 15% increase over last year's revenue by December 31st is an example of a well-defined goal.

Okay, now we have defined a goal. So how do making a right choice and goal setting mesh? Simply said, you need to CHOOSE YOUR PATH.

The famous New York Yankee all-star catcher (and later coach) Yogi Berra once said: "When you come to a fork in the road, take it!"

But which path should you choose?

When I was a young man working in television I went to see the President of Bonneville Communications, Arch Madsen. I asked him, "How do I develop a meaningful career in this business?"

He mentored me by giving a simple assignment. It was as follows:

Take 3 blank pages.

On page 1 write: Where do I want to *be* in…

3 months

6 months

1 year

2 years

5 years

10 years

On page 2 write: What skills must I *acquire* to be where I want to be in…

…and then include the same time frames.

Finally on page 3 write: What must I *do* to acquire the skills I need, to be where I want to be in…

…again including the same time frames.

"Then," he said, "every so often sit down and review your progress and make changes if necessary."

He knew full well plans were likely to change.

This exercise provides you with a *personal strategic plan* that is **S.M.A.R.T.!**

This plan really works if you pay attention to it.

Where Do I Want to *Be* in...

3 mo._____

_____

_____

6 mo._____

_____

_____

1 yr. _____

_____

_____

2 yr. _____

_____

_____

5 yr. _____

_____

_____

10 yr. _____

_____

_____

What Skills Must I *Acquire* to Be Where I Want to Be in...

3 mo. _____

_____

_____

6 mo. _____

_____

_____

1 yr. _____

_____

_____

2 yr. _____

_____

_____

5 yr. _____

_____

_____

10 yr. _____

_____

_____

What Must I *Do* to Acquire Skills I Need to Be Where I Want to Be in...

3 mo. _____

_____

_____

6 mo. _____

_____

_____

1 yr. _____

_____

_____

2 yr. _____

_____

_____

5 yr. _____

_____

_____

10 yr. _____

_____

_____

_____

Now that this is done you have hopefully chosen the right path (CTR) and have created a set of goals with a strategy to implement them.

So what are some of the obstacles we must tackle to travel the right path… the one that opens the funnel?

Number 1: **Embrace change!**

When the brilliant scientist Albert Einstein was asked during a press conference, "What are the constants in the universe?" he replied, "I only know of two. One is the speed of light and the other is change. And I'm not 100% sure about the speed of light!"

Change is a constant! Those that adapt and profit from positive change most often win.

Another scientist Charles Darwin is reputed to have espoused the idea of survival of the fittest, when in fact he developed a theory around the idea that those species which adapt best, thrive best. While we may or may not believe his theories, the idea that we must adapt in order to thrive is solid.

Not a day goes by without something in your life changing. What do you do about it? The best advice is to learn from it.

Let's imagine 150 years ago in the 1860s:

If a 747 jetliner landed in a field next to town, just how amazed and incredulous would the town people have been?

Now imagine 150 years into the future! What amazing things await us?

Or follow the path of electronics:

First it was radio with tube technologies, then transistors. Then came micro-chips and smaller devices. Eight-track players became cassettes and then mp3 players. Hard-wired speakers became blue tooth connected devices with great fidelity.

The list of rapid change goes on and on, and for some represents failing industries. To others, change brought opportunities to build entirely new and thriving industries.

Today's smartphone full of apps tells us more about the world we live in than a giant supercomputer of just 20 years ago.

So it is with life.

First we can barely move. Then we scoot, crawl, walk, then run. All along the way we manage the changes in our life without being fully aware of how rapidly they occur and what the impact might be.

Being fully aware of the change in your life—and being willing to find and develop the positive side—is your best strategy for success.

Number 2: **Embrace Resistance, make it work for you.**

Great athletes lift weights to increase performance. The really good ones relish these workouts!

Why? Because they increase performance!

Resistance training is an integral part of your development. It helps you by making you stronger. We need opposition to strengthen ourselves. Without it we don't fully appreciate the opportunity placed before us.

When we are forced to sample the bitter, we learn to savor the sweet. But when all we ever get is the sweet, it soon becomes unremarkable... even bland.

Not all resistance has to be physical. Much can be mental. Some can occur on the relationship side.

Many of the greatest stories of success tell of overcoming great adversity. These stories can be the most inspirational. Current and ancient history tell of those who fought their way through trials, and often errors on their path to success.

Along the way, coaches and mentors may apply pressure. This may not be pleasant. Just remember: if the coach is riding you, *it probably means the coach cares!*

A coach doesn't yell at the players he wants to *cut* from the team. He just cuts them!

If your mentor is giving you constructive criticism, it is a good sign you have promise. Listen and learn from these moments!

Number 3: **Approach each new challenge as an adventure!**

I remember my first job as a rookie account executive. Driving south on I-25 headed into Denver, I looked at the skyline and said, "Look at all those people I can call on!"

To some that challenge seemed daunting, but I had no book of business. Forced to make cold calls all day long, for me it was an adventure full of promise.

Each time you take on a new challenge, see it as a new adventure.

Of course for me, the most exciting adventure was the challenge of raising kids. Each one was a separate adventure. Soon my wife and I learned the number one rule of child raising: "They learn faster than you do!"

Now as I look back at 6 successful children and soon to be 16 grandchildren (so far), I cannot say enough about how important keeping an attitude of adventure contributes to a happy life.

Our children took us to places and adventures we would have never gone on our own. From peewee soccer games to high school competitions, from college to missions, we laughed, cheered, and wept for joy.

Later we danced at weddings, and were blessed to have grandchildren so we could watch the adventure all over again from the sideline.

Often people say the joy of grandchildren is that you can give them back.

I like to say the joy of grandchildren is watching them do to their parents what their parents did to you! But this time you get to wind them up!

Later in this book I'll share a few of the steps in raising children that I believe really work.

Number 4: **Learn something new every day.**

The legendary scientist Albert Einstein once said, "Imagination is more important than knowledge. Knowledge is limited, but imagination encircles the world."

When we begin to rest on the knowledge we have acquired we miss out on what might have been.

I have set a personal goal to learn a third language. That goal is specific, measurable, achievable, and time-bound. Meanwhile I am learning how to write books, paint with watercolors and use the next generation of digital media in business. Add to that the new skill sets that come with adapting to the aging process! I feel like I am 15 in my head—even if my body is in denial.

Imagine what you can do, what you can learn, what you might look forward to in the future. It stimulates and expands your world.

Those who do not expand their knowledge and imagination often find their world contracting around them. Don't let yourself miss the fun of each stage of life.

Number 5: **Serve others every day.**

I subscribe to the philosophy that: "When you push others down to look tall, you fight all the battles of a small person. But when you lift those around you, they will carry you out on their shoulders after the game!"

When you serve others unselfishly you may delay your rewards but you also elevate them.

There is an adage based on the golden rule that says: "What goes around comes around." I prefer "What comes around goes around."

If you send it out good, it will come back better. However, if you send it out bad it will come back *worse*.

When you make the CTR choice to serve, you gain friends, develop relationships, garner trust and your reputation will prosper.

In his sermon on the mount, Jesus said: "And whosoever shall compel thee to go a mile, go with him twain" (Matthew 5:41). Apparently there was a custom among the Roman occupiers that a Roman citizen could require a non-Roman to travel and carry his burdens. Jesus' advice meant that if you were asked to travel one mile with someone else, you should go a second and serve with free will. What might happen in that second mile?

First, the relationship of compulsion would be removed. Second, it is reasonable to assume a genuine friendship could evolve.

The lesson for us is simply that we acquire true friendship when we serve with free will. Our life is enriched.

Number 6: **Get an attitude of *Gratitude*.**

When we say thank you, something odd happens. Frequently people want to give more. They feel appreciated and often offer more without needing to be asked.

Take stock of how you are blessed and then seek out those who have helped you. This makes almost everyone more appreciative of you as a person. It also helps you take stock of the good things in your life and find a better attitude.

There is a saying that asks: "Is the glass half full or half empty?" My contention is the glass is always completely full. It may be half full of water but the other half is filled with air!

We need both air and water to survive. So take stock of the things in your life and how they help you. In doing so you will go through an attitude adjustment that yields positive effects.

Do you have friends who seem to be able to find the "dark lining to every silver cloud"? While they may be friends… unless you like to share their misery you should soon tire of their negativity.

Instead, show your gratitude. This attitude of gratitude fosters friendship and positive change.

Number 7: **Learn to laugh at yourself.**

There is a Riggleism that says, "When you make fun of yourself, you never have to worry about who you might have offended!"

Look inside yourself and realize that while some things are very important, many are not. There are those who perceive themselves to be better if they can run someone else down. The outcome of this behavior can be very sad.

There is a Biblical passage (Matthew 5:22) that says, "...Call ye no man fool." The scripture threatens a less than great outcome for the one who calls another a fool.

Instead take stock of yourself, be amused at your shortcomings and understand it is all about your personal growth. Learn to find amusement in your mistakes and delight in your success and you will be more fun to be around!

Number 8: **Understand that mistakes are part of the process.**

The Riggleism is: The only people that don't make mistakes aren't doing anything... and that may be the biggest mistake of all!

Some great people understood this concept, and put it to practice in their lives. We can learn from them. Thomas Edison, in his quest to create new and innovative ideas, failed many times, but yet did not consider himself a failure. He said, "I have not failed. I just found 10,000 ways that did not work."

Lucille Ball, entertainer and comedienne, opined, "I'd rather regret the things I've done, than regret the things I haven't done." The question is, what will *you* miss if you don't even try?

In Michael Jordan's case, he was cut from teams in his early career. But that didn't stop him. He said, "I can accept failure, everyone fails at something. But I can't accept not trying." Make that your mantra.

In the world we live in, our ability to rebound is important to our ultimate success.

So finally, "It's not how many times you get knocked down but how many times you get up again that counts!"

When you fail, grab your bootstraps and pull yourself up to find another way to solve the problem.

Number 9: **Accept the fact you cannot always make everyone happy. Instead just do what is right!**

Even when we are sure we have followed a correct path we may have our detractors. There are those who enjoy finding fault. It is easy to be drawn into a defensive mode by them and to get sidetracked in the process.

Instead, just do what you must to handle the problem. Rather than dwell on the criticism, focus instead on the positive outcome.

Set your sights on the direction of your goals and leave the detractors to wallow in negativity in their own little corners of the world.

In the end you are much more likely to win if you just *Choose the Right!*

Number 10: **Always, always take the high road.**

In the words of a children's song by the same name, just "Choose the Right" when a choice is placed before you!

Chapter 2
Make your House a Home Place!

When I managed a TV station in the southeast U.S., I was called to a conference in the very prestigious Florida home of the owner of the company. The home was magnificent. It had a hundred yards of private beach, a small ballroom, an elevator with phone service, and the master bedroom opened to the sea with a magnificent view.

The owner, unfortunately, had gone through a messy divorce and in the process disallowed the existence of his children.

As I sat in those magnificent surroundings I felt sad for him. He was obviously a successful man, but to me his house seemed empty!

A few weeks later my wife and I took our six children to the home of Floyd Henshaw. Floyd was a farmer who lived in an ancestral farmhouse. The house was "broken in" by years of family use from his children and grandchildren. The kitchen needed a remodel, the house needed a little paint. In the yard there was a huge tree with a tire swing. Our kids and his grandkids laughed and played.

Soon Floyd said, "Bring your kids to the barn." We did, and soon they were milking a cow! Each child took a turn and then we skimmed the cream and placed it in a hand-cranked ice cream maker.

As we enjoyed the fruit of our labors (including the fresh fruit he'd placed in the ice cream) Floyd gave us a bit of advice. "Riggle," he said in his deep southern drawl, *"you got to make your house a home place."*

So, what do you do to make your house a home place?

Here are a few tips, beginning with my beliefs about eleven family dynamics:

Dynamic 1:

We believe families will thrive in an environment of open and honest discussion.

This requires us to develop the skill of listening.

We are born with two ears but only one mouth. Learning to use them in that proportion will make everything work better.

Reflective listening is a skill that fosters communication. It also requires the artful use of a couple of questions:

"Let me see if I understood what you said. Did you say___?"

And, "When you said _____ what did you mean?"

Then listen and exchange thoughts.

Often when women speak they simply want to be heard. They are not looking for a guy to fix the problem.

It is smart to listen all the way to the end and then ask questions.

"Do you want me to do anything about it?"

Often the answer is, "No, I feel much better now."

Learning when *not* to speak is very important.

There are times when waiting for someone to get clear of a passionate outburst and then circling back later gets a better result.

With children, you must listen for meaning! (Refer to the reflective listening tip mentioned above.)

Often your partner may need to "detox" after a long hard day. Be sensitive to the moment and let that person have time alone in their "cave" before you try to communicate.

Dynamic 2:

Every Father and Mother should work in concert.

When referees at a football game throw a flag, if there are multiple flags for different violations they all come together to conference before announcing the penalty.

The players may even try to influence the decision by positioning themselves close to the referee conference.

The dynamic of parenting is often the same. While the parents may have a different outcome in mind, by taking the time to conference they can find a consistent solution.

Try a couple of simple rules:

A. Check with each other before making a final decision.
B. When one child says, "Mom said I could do this if you said it's okay..." stop and check with the partner just to make sure they haven't been told, "Dad said I could do this if you said it's okay." If possible, children will work both ends to get what they want.
C. Don't let the kids see you fight. Keep it private and off premises if possible.
D. If a decision is made, back your partner first and then discuss it privately.
E. When the younger child says, "You used to let my older brother or sister do this. Why can't I?" you can say, "because I learn from my mistakes!"

Remember children learn faster than you.

While they may not intentionally try to manipulate, their tendency is to do what works. Your responsibility is to manage the course.

Dynamic 3:

We believe you should never stop romancing your partner.

Were you taken the first time you met?

What made you want to be with your partner back then?

Now that you are together there's additional pressure of home expenses, and children's need for your attention. As the kids grow, their schedule demands more and more of your time. As you mature in your career (in and out of the home), you may end the day just wanting to relax and hide!

There are several things you can do to help keep the romance in your relationship:

1. Try to understand the other's point of view.
    Example: Read the word GO HANG A SALAMI. When spelled backwards the meaning is completely different. I'M A LASAGNA HOG.
    Same letters, same juxtaposition, but just one look from the opposite direction changes the entire meaning.
    Try to put yourself in your partner's position and listen with empathy and understanding.
    Then ask how you can help.
2. Give an unexpected surprise. Just because you brought home flowers doesn't need to mean you made a mistake. And if you don't have the money, just bring one flower. Or do something you know your partner will like.
3. Try to schedule a date every week. If you don't have money to go out, take a nice walk or just have a private picnic— but call it a date.

One of my most memorable dates was when I took my wife to a park. I spread a sheet on the table with votive candles and opened a picnic basket meal I had prepared on the sly. I brought music to play on a boom box. Since it was raining we sheltered under a pavilion and danced, just the two of us.

4. Schedule a periodic getaway. With money, stay somewhere nice, or without, just take a simple camping trip.

5. Hug and kiss, preferably in front of your kids (if you have them). It gives them a feeling of security!

6. Remember you are different. We were made that way. Celebrate the difference. As the French would say, "Vive la différence," or Long live the difference!

Dynamic 4:

We believe family council should discuss family issues in a problem solving way.

Schedule regular family councils. If you have a regular get together, or "Family Home Evening," create an atmosphere of discussion that allows family members to express their opinions without fear of criticism.

Once while in college (where I lived with 11 roommates in a house), I watched a fellow named Doug walk into the kitchen, up to a pressure cooker full of potatoes, and ask, "What's for dinner?" He proceeded to squeeze the handles of the pressure cooker and open it under full pressure. Of course it exploded and sent cooked potatoes exploding all over the walls and ceiling.

So it is with children. You have to let them vent sometimes, or later in life they will explode with undesirable behavior.

Enter the role of family council. The council provides a way to discuss issues, review choices, and talk about desired family activities.

Here are a few tips:

1. Use non-confrontational questions to direct the discussion.
2. Ask questions that cannot be answered yes or no, but require solutions.
3. Let everyone contribute to the agenda in a structured way. "What do you want to discuss in tonight's council?"
4. Create an atmosphere of discussion about choice.
   We used to say: "When you're young we make your decisions for you. When you get a little older you make

some of your decisions, and when you get into your late teens you make most of your own decisions. We prepare you for launch. Then finally we launch you and *you become responsible for your own choices*. We will then only help when you request it. So get ready for launch! Now, let's discuss some of your choices."

5. Set a structure for the council that includes some fun activity and refreshment, as well as house rules (decided of course in one of your councils).

6. Let respect be the guiding principle in these councils. Respect for the father and mother and the role of each child is essential.

    When things get out of hand use the code word "RESPECT!" to bring people back in line. Remind children you will respect their opinions if they respect your role as parents.

Dynamic 5: **We believe every child deserves a special position in the family.**

We had 6 children and each one evolved into a special role. In our family it was:

A. Oldest daughter, 1st of the clan, the writer.
B. Second daughter, creative specialist, musician, artist.
C. Our last little girl, precocious and precious.
D. Our first born son, the example, his brothers later called him the professor.
E. Our second son, "My Copy," and he still is to this day.
F. The beloved last son, our youngest treasure.

You should not want to position any child in a negative way. These positive designations guide their self-concept in a way that helps them progress.

Dynamic 6:

We believe every parent should create special time with each child.

As often as possible schedule some "alone time" with each and every child. Call it *their special time*!

It is always good to make it out of the house. It can be an expensive bit of entertainment or a simple trip to the dollar store. It can be a trip to the lake or somewhere you take interest in something they like.

It is during these visits you find special teaching moments or learn about their deepest feelings.

Dynamic 7:

We believe parents should teach the work ethic by working together with the children.

Working side by side with children provides unique teaching moments. By teaching them how to work, though labor intensive at first, eventually lightens your load.

This work can be in the yard, around the house, or even better, in the service of others.

I remember teaching the lesson of patience to my youngest son when we visited a rather grumpy and bossy older lady. She needed to be shoveled out from a major snow storm.

After her somewhat ungrateful ranting my son said, "Dad, why do you put up with that?"

I responded, "Son, for thirty minutes I can put up with almost anything… and it makes me appreciate your mom even more."

Later in his life while on a church mission in the Pacific he was able to practice the same principle.

The product of working side by side provides unique and—when done right—very fun moments.

Dynamic 8:

We believe families should build family traditions.

Vacations are a great starting point. Some of our most memorable moments have been built around family vacations.

I remember whitewater rafting where my wife fell out of the raft (everyone was shocked), a fishing trip and journey to Yellowstone, the time we rented the castle at Cub World and the little girls wore cone-shaped princess hats, and the time we rented a houseboat for a week. (Our kids still talk about that one).

Every year I took the boys to a private place where we held a Riggle-boy family campout. We tried to schedule a time and place where it was just us. We would Dutch oven cook, 4-wheel drive, and often fish. The final campout was with my youngest son after his older brothers had gone away to school. There was a fog in the valley and as we were making breakfast my good friend Bob— dressed in mountain man gear—came walking right out of the fog, black powder rifle on his shoulder and called out, "What's cookin' on the spit?" We then took time to eat steak and eggs and shoot black powder targets.

Our daughter scheduled a massive boy's food fight (à la Peter Pan) in her backyard complete with spray-can whipped cream. Later she put on a Victorian tea party (herbal) for the little girls, complete with fancy hats, ribbons, lace, and turn of the century decorations.

Every Christmas she schedules a gingerbread activity at our house. Last year eight separate houses were decorated by family and friends including, ten kids).

For years we bought items that represented the "12 Days of Christmas" song and dropped them on a selected family doorstep with an appropriate note, rang the doorbell and ran. Items included donuts for "5 Golden Rings," turtle candy for "Turtle Doves," and hardboiled eggs with French sayings written on them for "French Hens A-Laying," and so on. By the twelfth day you had to be like a stealth ninja to get away unseen. I will always remember our oldest son, dressed completely in black, having to jump into the branches of a tree and freeze like a ninja when the recipient family tried to catch him making his delivery. They looked straight at him, but couldn't see him. I still laugh about that moment.

These types of family traditions require planning and discussion. The family council is a great forum for creating lifelong memories.

The anticipation is almost as much fun as the event itself.

Dynamic 9:

We believe families should last longer and are more important than professional pursuits!

In my adult lifetime I have had 11 careers and different jobs. The one thing that persisted through it all was family.

The pursuit of career is important since it helps provide resources for a vibrant family life. Whether you work with a hundred employees or just yourself, a good family will be your most loyal asset.

A good friend of mine used to be the CEO of a substantial bank. His company merged twice with other banks, and he remained as CEO. Finally the bank was again bought out, and while he became the largest stockholder he was not to be the new CEO. In a friendly exchange I warned him, "When you're no longer CEO, you're likely to lose 75% of your friends, *because they'll be talking to your chair!* Just remember I am part of the 25%."

"You were wrong," he later said. "It's closer to 85%!"

The point of the story is that it's easy to be swayed by your professional success. While not everyone is so shallow, they still may want to share in the glow of your success. Meanwhile keep your head on straight and keep track of the "15%." Those friendships and family associations are worth more than millions!

Dynamic 10:

Learn to enjoy your surroundings no matter where you are.

In our travels my family has lived in Colorado, Texas, Oklahoma, Virginia, and Pennsylvania. We moved 11 times and enjoyed all of the places and long lasting friendships.

Challenge yourself to learn the local customs, history, and causes. Then adapt to your new environment—all the while staying true to your principles.

Dynamic 11:

Get inspired!

Whatever your faith, seek to understand and practice the true principles you find therein. Look for ways to help those around you. Avoid being judgmental and seek ways to give back to those you love. Find yourself in righteous places and run away from places that would take you down.

Remember it's easier to control yourself if you control your environment.

Talk to your Creator and seek truth. Find a way to honor your family and ancestors.

When you interface with others be gentle and persuasive to do right. Be genuine and honest. Seek pure knowledge and avoid hypocrisy. If you do these things your reward will be great!

To those who find hardship along the way, who are disappointed by their outcomes or those of their family, remember the words of Yankee catcher and hall of fame coach, Yogi Berra: "It ain't over till it's over!

Be patient and longsuffering. Practice the art of good choices and often the outcomes will change.

CHAPTER 3
Enjoy the Journey... Careers

At a recent dinner of the Pennsylvania Association of Broadcasters, the Gold award winner—Uke Washington, a prominent anchor talent in Philadelphia—made a couple of profound and relevant statements.

The first was: "It is not about the pursuit of happiness but rather the happiness in the pursuit."

The second statement was: "When you love your work you will never work a day in your life."

While not original these thoughts are profound. They speak to our attitude and how we approach our work. Even work that some consider drudgery can be made fun.

In my early life I had a summer job loading tractor trailer semis with stackable crates of bleach. Working side by side with my friend, we decided to race to see who could safely fill the trailer the fastest. We laughed and the competition was spirited... but we filled the trailers so fast the union steward told us to slow down. We were making others look bad! Our friendly game made the day go fast and we became stronger because of the strenuous workout.

So here a few pointers on how to enjoy the journey we call a career:

1. *Try to learn something new every day.*

   Each day is not complete until you learn something new. If you think you already know all there is to know, you're probably making a mistake.

   A couple of famous quotes give us guidance.

   The famous artist and inventor Leonardo da Vinci understood this concept when he said, "Learning never exhausts the mind." When we set our path toward learning we only help ourselves.

   In our day Lou Holtz, the famous football coach and TV commentator, said, "I never learn anything by talking. I only learn things when I ask questions." There is no doubt that asking questions opens the door to learning.

2. *Make your handshake your bond.*

   Walter Annenberg, publisher of *TV Guide,* made a deal to sell WPVI (a privately owned ABC powerhouse television station) to ABC corporate television. In those days it took almost a year to close on such a transaction. During those twelve months the book value of WPVI grew substantially. When the station was about to close, the President of ABC approached Mr. Annenberg and asked if he wanted to discuss the valuation. Walter Annenberg responded, "We shook hands on it, didn't we? The deal still stands."

   As the ABC president was later introducing Walter Annenberg, he said, "I would take a handshake from this man over a contract from any of you!"

How much is that kind of a reputation worth? Clearly Walter Annenberg didn't need any more money—he was already a billionaire—but his reputation meant a lot to him.

So let it be said of you, your handshake of agreement is your bond.

3. *Don't be afraid of dirty jobs!*

For eight years Mike Rowe starred in a television series on the Discovery Channel called "Dirty Jobs." In 2013 he began his second series, "Somebody's Got to Do It!" on CNN. In these shows Mr. Rowe featured the ugliest of jobs that needed to be done in order to bring various products to market.

In so doing he created a strong career for himself and an interesting position in the marketplace. In short, his lack of fear of dirty jobs made him a nice career and plenty of money.

In football the role of a linebacker is to fill a hole. It is a tough job and requires plenty of preparation and training. If there was no one willing to fill the hole, the team would lose the game.

On a kickoff the receiving team often forms a blocking wedge to help the return specialist move up the field. On defense there are assigned players who have the task of running down and charging into and dislodging the wedge so the other players can tackle the runner. There is not a lot of glory in this assignment but it is vital if the team is to win.

So ask yourself this question: "Am I willing to take on the tough jobs?" What do you think your company's leadership thinks about people who are willing to take on the dirty jobs? Your willingness to take the tough assignments may serve you well.

4. ***Remember you are being paid for a certain job and you need to find out what it is.***
Despite what you may think, nobody owes you a job. You have to earn it. Work hard to determine what is expected.

The historic story teller Mark Twain once said: "Don't go around saying the earth owes you a living. The earth owes you nothing. It was here first."

5. ***Understand where you stand on the mountain.***
If you liken a company/organization to a large mountain with the CEO/Boss at the top and workers at different elevations, you realize your view from the valley may not be as expansive as the view from the peak. But your job is to take care of business at your level.

Realize that, according to your perspective, those who have a wider vision may sometimes ask you to do things you don't understand. Respect their requests, but do not be afraid to offer insight from your vantage point that can supplement their view so you can both better do your jobs.

When you do this effectively, you will often find you have moved up the mountain.

6. ***Be happy for the success of others—not jealous!***

There are times when others have great success because of serendipity and then there are times when hard work pays off. In these times it is easy to say, "Why didn't that happen to me?"

This attitude can work against you. If you get caught up in negative thoughts it can slow your own progress. Instead be happy for their success and learn from it. Instead say, "Isn't this a great country?"

This attitude will make you a better person and provide valuable learning moments.

7. *Respect the labor of your fellow workers.*

When they do well, no matter how menial the task, recognize your co-workers' achievement and tell them you appreciate the quality of what they do. In so doing you often turn them into an ally who will help you along your own path.

8. *Don't let your personal life become a part of your work. Keep them separate and be professional.*

Enough said!

9. *Try to build those around you.*

Again the Riggleism: "When you push down those around you to make yourself look tall, you fight all the battles of a small person. But when you build those around you they will carry you out on the shoulders when the game is over."

When you help others grow, you help yourself.

This principle is hard to explain but really works. You create friendships, and build trust. There is a reward in seeing others succeed even when they might not realize how much you helped.

10. *Remember, good fortune seems to favor the well prepared.*

While there is something to be said for the ability to improvise and think on your feet, nothing replaces proper preparation.

Take the time to get ready and anticipate oncoming change.

Approach each new task with a strategy and surprise yourself with the good luck you will find!

Abraham Lincoln said, "Things may come to those who wait, but only what's left from those who hustle."

Prepare well, with a good strategy, then hustle to make it happen and good fortune will follow you around.

11. *Don't be afraid of difficult or duplicitous people. They sometimes could use a little help too.*

You may be forced to deal with them.

The Riggleism for this reads: "You can walk among the snakes. Just remember to wear tall boots and carry a long forked stick."

Another life lesson came to me when a dear friend and I had a philosophical discussion. I said, "Some of the most important and difficult decisions come while you are walking in a gray area."

He replied, "There are no gray areas. Everything is black or white, right or wrong!"

I countered, "Look closely at this newspaper photograph. You are right, it is made only of little tiny black dots on white paper. But what if I asked you to walk only in the white areas without stepping in the black?"

When forced to confront the gray areas, *choose the right*. You will feel what is right and what is not. You may have to slog through areas that are less than desirable… but if you choose well, you will do well.

Chapter 4
The Joy of Leadership.

With a little good fortune and preparation we end up having the challenge of leading others. This opportunity requires a whole new set of skills that aren't always taught.

To lead we first need to change the way we think.

In a speech to graduating Brazilian students, genius Albert Einstein said, "Thinking is to man what flying is to birds. Don't follow the example of the chickens when you could be like the lark."

So how do we change our thinking to better lead, to fly like the lark?

Consider "Share of Mind and Heart"…

In the late 700s in southern France, a great walled castle city on the hill of Carsac was occupied by the Moors. The woman in charge was Dame Carcass. In the later part of the decade Charlemagne decided it was necessary to capture the city because of its strategic location—central to Paris, Spain and Italy. So he sent an invading army.

The city was so well provisioned and protected by walls that Charlemagne's army could not get in (see Figure 4.1).

A five-year siege began. Eventually, provisions began to run low. Dame Carcass said, "Bring me a small pig and a bag of grain." She then fed the pig so much grain its belly became distended.

Figure 4.1—Carcassone (photo credit Ad Meskens)

Soldiers took the overfed pig and threw it from the tall rampart walls. When it hit the ground it burst and the grain spewed out on the ground.

When the leaders of the invading army saw this, they decided to leave. If the castle town could still afford to feed grain to its pigs after a five-year siege, they obviously were in for nothing but a longer wait.

As they departed Dame Carcass rang a bell (the French verb is *sonner*) which signaled the invaders to come back for a conference. They did and both parties worked out an agreement where everybody could win.

Later the city was called "Carcassonne" (Lady Carcass Rings).

This true story illustrates the power of *Share of Mind.*

When you lead any group of people it is best if you can capture this share of mind.

We'll talk about that in more detail later, but first let's discuss the second part of good leadership: capturing *Share of Heart.*

There is a body of research that suggests there are three key areas of the brain which affect the choices we make: the Neo Cortex, Limbic and Autonomic.

The Neo Cortex processes logical decision making, the Autonomic processes automatic functions such as breathing and the like.

But the magic Limbic section of your brain makes emotional decisions. These emotional decisions can occur up to 8-10 times faster than the logical ones.

Most people first make Limbic or emotional decisions then use the Neo Cortex to logically justify that decision. So when you are fortunate to lead, it is paramount you understand *why* your group chooses to follow you.

More often than not, they follow because they have emotionally bought into your leadership. They have made a Limbic, or emotional choice.

This is why companies use mission statements. It is also why many companies seek feedback from their staff—to develop "buy in" to the process.

Learning to manage these emotional choices is an art.

First, you have to understand the motivation of your direct reports—what makes them have passion for their work.

Then you have to manage the structure that helps them fulfill the assigned but hopefully "bought-into" task.

And finally, you have to understand those followers have the power of choice to continue to follow, or *not* follow. You must articulate and even sell the company/organization mission, and the task that needs to be done to move ahead.

Often what seems to be a thoughtfully designed program just never seems to get any traction. Why? Because employees without "buy-in" use passive resistance. They find a way to delay, to not play. If they have not fully "bought-in" the task seems most difficult.

Occasionally, you will need to offer the choice of, "It needs to be done. If you can't do it, we can find somebody who *will*."

While sometimes necessary, this approach requires a lot more work. This form of Limbic or emotional management is not always as much fun.

At a training conference of business unit leaders in Orlando, Florida, I had the good fortune of learning how to manage creative people from the division head of the Disney Company who managed creative staff.

He brought a jazz ensemble on stage and explained that the players decide ahead of time to break the music into 16-measure segments. Each ensemble member gets a turn to star during their segment. The piano player freelances the melodic line for his 16 measures, then the saxophonist takes a turn while the rest of the ensemble moves to supporting roles. Next it's the percussionist's turn. Then the trombone player and so forth.

At the end we were entertained and the players were happy.

After the musical display finished, our instructor said:

"When you manage creative people, you must first decide on the parameters and then let them work within those same parameters."

So it is when you have staff. When possible you must define the expected parameters (sometimes together, sometimes directed) and then give employees the responsibility to work and even shape their labor inside those parameters.

When you can do this effectively, you will have motivated, productive people who take pride in their part of the workplace "melody."

That's when you have captured *Share of Heart!*

SHARE OF MIND

What is the difference between a standard black baseball cap and the same hat with a little Nike swoosh on it? The answer is about $20.

Why do a dozen Top Flight golf balls cost $12 when a dozen Titleist Pro V 1 golf balls cost $45? While there may be a difference in the way the golf ball performs it is doubtful (at least to me) the golf ball is four times better.

On one occasion I was lucky enough to hit a hole-in-one. I took the golf ball and had it framed and mounted on my office wall.

Then the thought came: I got a hole-in-one using a Top Flight Ball. If I used the Pro V 1 ball, would I have been four times more likely to sink it in one? Or would I have four times as many holes-in-one?

Sometimes we purchase or react to a situation based on perception. The truth of the matter is, gaining *Share of Mind*, or positioning, does lend value to the process. So it is with your workers. If they perceive or believe your work has intrinsic value they will present it that way.

Part of your role is to present *Share of Mind*—or brand or market position—to your own staff so they enhance the way your image is presented. If employees take a certain pride of ownership in the company, and they feel the company is an excellent employer with useful products or services, they will be more effective workers.

Since we all must sell something (including our own value to the company) we must focus on our USP—Unique Selling Proposition.

What is it that makes you unique and better? What do you have that is special and of value to your customers?

When you can train your staff to position your best attributes they will exude that *Share of Mind*.

Everybody wants to work for a great enterprise.

Your role as a leader is to teach and coach your employees toward this *Share of Mind*, and then create an environment where they develop *Share of Heart*.

Then the true joy of leadership emerges.

Leadership Rules of Engagement

Once you have established *Share of Mind* and *Share of Heart* with your staff, it may be time to consider how you engage in leading your enterprise.

Unfortunately, hardly anyone wants to be on a team that doesn't have a winning culture. As a result a few concepts may apply:

Concept 1.

Before you can deal with reality, you must first deal with perceptions.

Take the time to sort out the perceptions. Ask good non-confrontational questions that will get you honest answers. Find out what your customers think, and more importantly what your employees think.

This can be done with customer surveys, internal facilitators, or just plain old common sense.

I always subscribed to the idea of MBWA—Managing By Wandering Around. Twice each day I would leave my office and walk around the building asking questions.

I learned a lot from my employee base of about 100 workers. I wondered if the principle would apply on a bigger scale.

In a corporate training session for leaders of businesses with over $5 billion in annual sales, we were treated to a session with the former CEO of Pepsico, a company with over 250k employees. He reinforced my style with an upgrade—he called it Management by *Wondering* Around. He would take the time to go into his many business units and walk the floor at the "boots on the ground" level. He stated it often changed the company at the corporate level.

So spend the time and effort to survey your customers inside and outside your business.

Concept 2.

Part of being smart is knowing when you are not, and then surrounding yourself with people who are.

Assembling the right team is an art form. Find people who are not only smart but also wise.

I like to call it "street smart."

Considerable effort goes into recruiting and drafting players to professional sport teams. Finding the right player for each task is critical but should also be driven by the needs of that task.

The same is true in your organization. It's great to have the money to "buy" talent but it's not always affordable. So what do you do? This question takes us to the next concept.

Concept 3.

Listen to and look for good coaches...

Even the best pro golfers use swing and strategy coaches. Why shouldn't you?

Coaches can help take your current talent to the next level. Coaches are often people who have been in the position before and have insight only available from the inside. While they may not be able to perform as well as in former days, their skill sets are more valuable than ever.

These coaches are often very well suited to find and train new "potentials."

Concept 4.

Between the stripes, it is helmets and pads. On the sidelines we can be friends but on the field it's a competition for customers.

Competition is the life blood of the free enterprise system. When we compete we are often forced to innovate and make positive change.

Teach those who report to you that friendly competition is part of your culture. This requires you to know your competition. Appropriate surveys of the competitive style of operation and knowledge of how they sell against you is important.

Find out how your competitors sell themselves and know how they compare to you. Then you can fashion an offense to move forward with a better position and brand, while creating an internal culture that helps you win.

After all if we are not playing to win, then why do we keep score?

Concept 5.

Risk assessment. Ask yourself, "What do I have to lose? And what do I have to gain?"

When undertaking a new effort. These questions are important. It is critical to STOP and assess the possible losses and gains so you can carefully decide how they will affect your company or organization or staff.

Sometimes the biggest risk is not to take a risk.

However, entire careers are devoted to risk assessment and learning when to take—and not take—the risk is very important.

Concept 6.

Learn to fly high cover!

If business marketing can be likened to warfare, then developing a good strategy is critical.

Using this analogy we can assume there is an element of ground soldiers or "boots on the ground" marketing staff.

They do the difficult, often tactical part, of your revenue development. They interface with the customer and use the company assets to solve customer problems. In so doing they create revenue possibilities.

As leader, your role can be to work with them in the ground marketing war. But more important is learning to fly "high cover." Much like an air force who clears the way so ground soldiers can proceed with greater efficiency, your role is to clear obstacles to your team's progress.

Make sure the organization is supportive of each person's role and while working inside assigned parameters that the systems which support them are efficient.

Make sure customer service is responsive to company promises and when necessary, understand that flexibility is just as important as rules.

Learn to listen to the genius of your "boots on the ground" troops and they will show you how to clear impediments to progress.

Concept 7.

Teach proper use of the LIGHT Saber!

In the *Star Wars* movies, the hero Jedi Knights are issued a powerful light saber that, when used with "The Force," allows them to defeat many forms of adversarial weaponry. Jedi Knights require intensive training and knowledge that the saber is to be used only when necessary (at least by the good guys).

In real life, leadership carries its own form of light saber, or power sword. The higher you sit in the hierarchy of the organization the more powerful your saber—and the more careful you have to be not to use it without necessity.

As new people come on board, they are often issued small light sabers in the form of power to implement. Occasionally these new members draw their sabers and start slashing around. In this instance you may have to use your saber to remind them not to improperly use theirs.

Your job as a leader is to train them how and *when* to properly use it. The careful and judicious use is to get things done. Teach them why it is issued in the first place, and let them know that as they properly use the resource, it becomes more powerful.

Sometimes a staff member will be unable to get something done in conjunction with another person or institution. In a fit, that person will ask you to use *your* sword to their end. At such times it is wise to point out that if you use your sword for their gain only, it will likely create animosity and perhaps even retaliation. Advise them to go work out the problem together and if it still cannot be resolved, to bring the issue back to you, together.

Such use of your power will more often than not create good relationships inside the company. Exercise a steady hand and judicious use of your own power saber.

You will actually be flying "high cover."

Concept 8.

Build your direct reports. When you have recruited well it is not uncommon to have people who set their sights on someday having your job.

This can be a great thing!

Remember you are the coach and having capable players on your team helps you—and actually can make your life easier.

There may be days when it is easier to "just do it yourself," but it trains employees to offload their issues in your office, letting them put the "monkey on your back" after you had assigned it to them.

Instead take the time to coach and teach your staff how to deal with the problem. Teach them the things *they don't know they don't know.*

Eventually your load will lighten and you will be respected.

Remember, you want your team to carry you out on their shoulders when the game is over.

Chapter 5
Enjoy the Sunset!

Change is a constant!

Things that used to be easy to do, now hurt.

Our body's metabolism slows down and tasty food we used to enjoy without consequence now goes to all the wrong places.

Like me, you may be 15 years old in your head but your body is in total denial. A trip to the doctor becomes a social event.

Sounds terrible. Right?

Wrong!

What you need is an attitude adjustment! Start with the knowledge that *they don't put a luggage rack on a coffin!*

Getting old is not a privilege afforded to everyone.

In my early years I spent a great deal of time in the pursuit of athletic activities. In college I was a member of the university volleyball team and would practice or play for about four hours each day.

After I was married with family I played competitive tournament ball. But something happened. I began to get old. I graduated to coed leagues, then senior leagues, then nobody-wants-me leagues.

It was very frustrating, since in my head I knew the skills—but when it came to executing those same skills my body was in total denial.

Then I had a mentor moment.

While visiting a friend in the hospital who was recuperating from a knee operation, I voiced my frustration.

He wisely said, "Let it go! Find something you can do and learn to enjoy that instead."

So I pursued racquetball for a while and then golf and then walking and so on. Each step of the way I learned or appreciated something new.

As a child I would go to the lake and swim and splash around. Now when I go to the lake I sit with my wonderful wife and partner and just enjoy the sunset.

Then the blessing of grandchildren came along. (We are soon to have our 16th). There is a common saying among grandparents that the beauty of grandchildren is you can give them back. I like to give it an additional spin.

To reiterate: **The beauty of grandchildren is... they do to their parents what their parents did to you! And *you* get to wind them up...**   It's a wonderful thing.

Grandparenting is a spectator sport.

While you want to intercede—because you may know how to handle situations—you should not (unless asked).

Recently one of my daughters-in-law sent this message.

"Grandpas teach grandchildren mischief they have not yet thought of."

It is true.

I used to love going fishing all by myself. Now I enjoy baiting, untangling and watching kids catch the big fish, so much more than just fishing! The youthful excitement of catching the first fish or the wonderment of the nature that surrounds it is pure fun!

In fact part of this reset is you appreciate the struggles of others and understand their trials so much more than they can imagine. When they do come to you for advice it is very validating.

For fun, once in a while, look at a promising young person who struggles with who they are, what they will become, and what is in their future and say to yourself… "Man am I glad I don't have to do that again!"

Remember change is a constant. Embrace it. Make it into something great and new. Develop new hobbies and skills that use your wisdom and experience. It's okay to accept the fact you can't do some things you used to do. Find something else because this part of the journey can be fun too.

To those *who will listen,* teach and coach.

Maybe they can skip some of the mistakes you made.

Build yourself a new set of goals by:

1. Doing the three sheets of paper exercise mentioned earlier in this book.

   Sheet one: Where do I want to *be*...

   Sheet two: What skills must I *acquire*...

   Sheet three: What must I *do* to acquire those skills to be where I want to be....

2. Set S.M.A.R.T. goals every year and post them in a prominent place. Revise them when necessary.

3. Remember to laugh at yourself often.

4. Learn something new every day.

5. Measure blessings and be thankful for them.

6. Learn to find the good side to everything... *Even a dark cloud can have a silver lining,* if you just know how to look for it.

7. Treasure your true friendships.

Most important of all... Make your house a home place!

About the Author

John Riggle graduated from Brigham Young University in 1971 with a bachelor's degree in Communications, and minors in Sociology, French, and Physical Education.

He has been married to Marlene Riggle more than 40 years (which qualifies her for sainthood). No doubt his fluency in French helped woo her.

John has worked in top management positions at four television stations and has a distinguished career in marketing. He serves on the board of Pennsylvania Association of Broadcasters and is a past board chairman and broadcaster of the year. In addition, he has served on more than 20 non-profit boards, and in a variety of leadership positions in his church for nearly 50 years.

John Riggle's leadership in business, non-profit, civic and church groups forms the basis of wisdom you can apply immediately. But most importantly, with 6 successful children and soon to be 16 grandchildren, he offers humor and hands-on tips you can use to create your own long and successful marriages and families.

www.ingramcontent.com/pod-product-compliance
Lightning Source LLC
Chambersburg PA
CBHW071631040426
42452CB00009B/1579